Vatican II: Act II

An Adult Discussion Program

Robert L. Kinast

FAMILIES

Participant's Guide

A Program of The National Pastoral Life Center

 THE LITURGICAL PRESS
Collegeville, Minnesota

While the authors and editors of *Vatican II: Act II* are sensitive to the use of inclusive language, they did not deem it proper to alter the wording of the documents of Vatican II and Scripture used in this book.

Fr. Robert L. Kinast, director of the Center for Theological Reflection, Madeira Beach, Florida, is the principal author of this discussion program.

Cover design by Don Bruno.

Nihil obstat: Joseph C. Kremer, Th.D. *Censor Deputatus.*
Imprimatur: ✝ Jerome Hanus, O.S.B., Bishop of St. Cloud, September 4, 1990.

ISBN 0-8146-1972-X

Contents

Foreword

"It is in relation to Vatican II that modern Catholics live their faith, whether they realize it or not. Vatican II is the point of reference for the modern Catholic Church." How significant this quotation from *Vatican II: Act II*. The Second Vatican Council has truly become part of the air we breathe.

A significant aspect of that change of climate brought on by Vatican II is the communal nature of the Church. Perhaps in no way has the Second Vatican Council become a more meaningful point of reference for Catholics than in the way parishioners today experience community in the Sunday Eucharist, in the other sacramental celebrations, and in the growing number of small faith sharing communities that have sprung up around the world.

Small communities alone enjoy a remarkably different role and acceptance in the scheme of parish life today as compared to thirty years ago. Once engaged in by "Catholic Action types" at the periphery of the parish, they now involve a healthy percentage of parishioners in the mainstream of parish life.

So accepted has the value of small communities come to be that in *Small Christian Communities: A Vision of Hope* those of us who have worked with RENEW recently identified three types of small groups and communities for which we offer practical organizing advice. *Seasonal small groups* foster the spiritual growth of large numbers of parishioners; *ministerial communities* offer a strong base for all ministry; and *small Christian communities* call for a deep commitment to a holistic spirituality that seeks to transform all of life and society.

The support for small communities in parishes truly calls for a great amount of care and nurturing. On several counts *Vatican II: Act II* fits the bill well. Designed specifically for use by popular seasonal groups, it enables them to move past reflections that tend to linger on personal piety. Parishioners will be challenged to move beyond the level of personal comfort in their seasonal group to respond to Vatican II's call to responsible involvement and evangelization. *Vatican II: Act II* will do the same for ministerial communities as they see their call in faith to embrace substantially more than the ministry of their choosing. For small Christian communities it will provide the substance for study that enables enlightened decisions and sound actions for connecting the gospel and the marketplace.

In all of this *Vatican II: Act II* gives us a wealth of much needed material that provides for solid small group and small community growth. What finer source of ideas and formation than the very teachings and guidance of the Church in council? What surer way to know that directions taken are inspired by the Holy Spirit? Small Christian communities offer great hope for the future. They contribute to a vision that gives us an ideal to move toward as we enter the third millennium. *Vatican II: Act II* takes a fine stride in the right direction of enabling that vision to walk.

Rev. Msgr. Thomas A. Kleissler
Founder and Director of RENEW

Introduction

VATICAN II

Vatican II was a series of meetings of all the Roman Catholic bishops of the world, convened by the Pope. Such meetings are called "general" or "ecumenical" (worldwide) councils. Prior to Vatican II there had been only twenty such councils in the history of the Church.

Vatican II lasted from 1962 to 1965. The meetings themselves were held in the fall, usually beginning in October and ending in December. The council was called by Pope John XXIII, who died after the first session, and was concluded by Pope Paul VI.

The overall purpose of the council was to examine the Church in order to renew its internal life, support the movement for Christian unity (ecumenism), and contribute to the solution of problems in the modern world.

The most tangible result was the sixteen documents the council produced. These consist of four constitutions, which discuss theological issues; nine decrees, which present principles for Church action; and three declarations, which discuss issues outside the Church.

The council documents set forth the vision and direction of the Church. This is not a single, uniform vision but a combination of viewpoints, of many sources of spiritual energy that seek constantly to work together. Subsequent documents and developments find their basis in these documents of Vatican II.

The official name of each document is taken from the first words in its Latin text. The documents, together with their English titles and main themes, are listed at the back of this book.

The council has had a far-reaching impact, described here under four headings:

Postconciliar documents. Numerous documents have been produced since the council to implement, clarify, or develop the principles set down by Vatican II, especially those regarding liturgy and ecumenism. A sampling of the postconciliar documents is found in the two volumes *Vatican Council II: The Conciliar and Post Conciliar Documents* and *Vatican Council II: More Post Conciliar Documents*, published by The Liturgical Press, Collegeville, Minnesota.

Structures. In order to implement the vision of Vatican II, new structures have been developed. These include national conferences of bishops, priests' councils, and diocesan and parish pastoral councils. To continue worldwide consultation between the Pope and the bishops, synods of bishops are held approximately every three years, with a representative number of bishops from every country attending.

Priorities. Today, spirituality is fostered through liturgy more than through personal devotions, and within the liturgy emphasis is on participation rather than on mere attendance. Scripture is more central than catechism; an ecumenical spirit of openness and cooperation is evident in relations with other Christians; the laity are seen as equal partners with clergy and religious in the ministry of the Church; concern for the poor of our society is cultivated through action for social change rather than through charity alone.

Experiences. Closely aligned with new priorities are new experiences of being Catholic. Among these is the experience of community, often nurtured in small groups that have a prayer-sharing focus. In like manner, the experience of liturgy, of the clergy, of adult faith, of other Christians and other religions, of social commitment, have all been affected by Vatican II. It is in relation to Vatican II that modern Catholics live their faith, whether they realize it or not. Vatican II is the point of reference for the modern Catholic Church.

VATICAN II: ACT II

Vatican II: Act II provides a format for studying the Vatican II documents, reflecting on the impact they continue to have, and responding to the Church's challenge to action. The six-session program is for adults who are serious about living as Catholics in today's world under the influence of Vatican II. It is designed to keep the vision of Vatican II alive by recalling its message and relating it to contemporary experience.

The present topic, *Families,* looks at the theme of family as lived out in both two-parent nuclear families and single-parent families, and the related topic of parenting within the Christian context and of youth as valued contributors to society. We examine what Vatican II said as well as our response to the council's message. Important to the program is the concept that learning must lead to action; both learning and action are stressed throughout. An optional seventh session is included, designed for planning and carrying out an action based on the group's understanding of Vatican II principles.

After completing *Families,* groups could decide to begin another six-session program.

Vatican II: Act II is meant to be used by small groups meeting in the parish or in the homes of members. Each session is designed for an hour-and-a-half time period, plus about a half-hour preparation time for the session. Each participant should have a copy of the *Participant's Guide*. The group leader should have a copy of the *Convener's Guide* and should be prepared to lead the discussions.

Family Life Today: An Overview

Goals

- To share the group's experience of family life today
- To share what the group thinks the Church's role in family life should be
- To recall that Vatican II spoke of family life in terms of marriage, parenting, youth, and special marriage situations
- To put this learning into practice through action

Scripture

As we begin to consider family life, we hear Jesus tell us what it takes to be part of his family.

Mark 3:31-35 **His mother and his brothers arrived. Standing outside they sent word to him and called to him. A crowd seated around him told him, ''Your mother and your brothers [and your sisters] are outside asking for you.'' But he said to them in reply, ''Who are my mother and [my] brothers?'' And looking around at those seated in the circle he said, ''Here are my mother and my brothers. [For] whoever does the will of God is my brother and sister and mother.''**

Prayer

May the Virgin Mary, who is the mother of the Church, be a mother to the Church in our homes. May St. Joseph, the guardian of the Holy Family, help us care for the families entrusted to us. May Jesus, who learned his first human lessons in a family, enlighten our learning about families today. We ask this through the same Christ our Lord. Amen.

—Based on The Christian Family in the Modern World, no. 86

Our Experience of Family

TYPES OF FAMILIES

We usually don't think of ''family'' in terms of ''type.'' But we have all known different types of families. To see how many we have known, put a check next to the types of families you have lived in and an X next to those you have known but not lived in.

_____*Nuclear family* (father and mother permanently married, father employed, mother at home)

_____*Extended family* (other relatives living with nuclear family)

_____*Single-parent family* (divorce, death, non-marriage)

_____

_____

This quotation from Pope John Paul II's apostolic exhortation The Christian Family in the Modern World will probably add types of families we haven't thought of:

> It is necessary to call special attention to certain particular groups which are more in need not only of assistance but also of more incisive action upon public opinion and especially upon cultural, economic and juridical structures, in order that the profound causes of their needs may be eliminated as far as possible.
>
> Such for example are the families of migrant workers; the families of those obliged to be away for long periods, such as members of the armed forces, sailors and all kinds of itinerant people; the families of those in prison, of refugees and exiles; the families in big cities living practically speaking as outcasts; families with no home; incomplete or single-parent families; families with children that are handicapped or addicted to drugs; the families of alcoholics; families that have been uprooted from their cultural and social environment or are in danger of losing it; families discriminated against for political or other reasons; families that are ideologically divided; families that are unable to make ready contact with the parish; families experiencing violence or unjust treatment because of their faith; teenage married couples; the elderly, who are often obliged to live alone with inadequate means of subsistence (no. 77).

CHURCH AND FAMILIES

Given the many types of families today, what are the three most important things the Church can do to strengthen family life?

1. _____

_____

_____

2. _____

_____

_____

3. _____

_____

_____

In your experience, when has the Church been most helpful and least helpful to families?

Most Helpful: _____

_____

_____

Least Helpful: _____

_____

_____

Vatican II Speaks

Vatican II spoke of families in several of its documents, especially in the ones listed below:

Dogmatic Constitution on the Church (nos. 11, 35)
Decree on the Pastoral Office of Bishops in the Church (no. 12)
Decree on the Training of Priests (no. 2)
Decree on the Apostolate of Lay People (nos. 11, 30)
Decree on the Church's Missionary Activity (no. 15)
Declaration on Christian Education (no. 3)
Declaration on Religious Liberty (no. 5)

The most complete treatment, however, was in Part II, Chapter 1, Pastoral Constitution on the Church in the Modern World.

In addition, the 1980 synod of bishops, representing the countries of the world, discussed family life, and after the synod, in 1981 Pope John Paul II issued an apostolic exhortation, The Christian Family in the Modern World.

In the coming weeks we will discuss family life under four general headings: Marriage, Parenting, Youth, and Special Marriage Situations. We will share our experience, learn from the council and the Pope, and listen to one another—all with the goal of seeing what we can do to contribute to family life in our own situation: neighborhood, parish, school, community, workplace.

Summing Up

Vatican II spoke of family life in terms of marriage, parenting, youth, and special marriage situations. Our discussion listed many different types of families.

What did I learn about families that was new to me, particularly striking, or helpful?

_____

_____

_____

To make this learning practical, answer this question:

How can I put what I have learned into practice in my daily life?

_____

_____

_____

Action

To carry out my responsibility as a member of the people of God, I can join the effort within my parish or diocese to give help to families in need—with transportation, tutoring, child care, and the like—according to my own gifts.

To help improve conditions for families in need, I can find out what kinds of public assistance are available to families in need, and I can contact the elected officials to urge better services.

Before the Next Session

Try to carry out one of the Action suggestions.

Complete your answers to the Summing Up questions if you did not have a chance to do so during the session itself.

Complete the statement ''In my view the most important point about Christian marriage is . . .'' on page 19 in the next session.

Read the section Vatican II Speaks on pages 19–21.

Read the Home Study Questions for this session on pages 15–17, and read the Home Study Questions for Session 2, pages 22–24; or read Part II, Chapter 1, Pastoral Constitution on the Church in the Modern World.

Closing Prayer   **O God, you continually renew our Christian families by the faith and love of our members and the sacraments of the Church. Help us to act as a family in our service to the parish and neighboring community. We ask this through Christ our Lord. Amen.**

> —Based on Pope John Paul II's exhortation
> The Christian Family in the Modern World, no. 50

Home Study Questions   **BALANCED VIEW**

Sometimes it seems like the Church emphasizes the negative experiences of marriage. Does it have anything positive to say about marriage?

Vatican II tried to be both realistic and positive:

> Christians today are overjoyed, and so too are all who esteem conjugal and family life highly, to witness the various ways in which progress is being made in fostering those partnerships of love and in encouraging reverence for human life; there is progress too in services available to married people and parents for fulfilling their lofty calling: even greater benefits are to be expected and efforts are being made to bring them about (Pastoral Constitution on the Church in the Modern World, no. 47).

The council spoke also of negative elements within marriage:

> This happy picture of the dignity of these partnerships is not reflected everywhere, but is overshadowed by polygamy, the plague of divorce, so-called free love, and similar blemishes; furthermore, married love is too often dishonored by selfishness, hedonism, and unlawful contraceptive practices. Besides, the economic, social, psychological, and civil climate of today has a severely disturbing effect on family life. There are also the serious and alarming problems arising in many parts of the world as a result of population expansion (no. 47).

Pope John Paul II further discussed these positive and negative aspects of marriage:

> On the one hand, in fact, there is a more lively awareness of personal freedom and greater attention to the quality of interpersonal relationships in marriage, to promoting the dignity of women, to responsible procreation, to the education of children. There is also an awareness of the need for . . . reciprocal spiritual and material assistance, the rediscovery of the ecclesial mission proper to the family and its responsibility for the building of a more just society. On the other hand, however, signs are not lacking of a disturbing degradation of some fundamental values: a mistaken theoretical and practical concept of the independence of the spouses in rela-

tion to each other; serious misconceptions regarding the relationship of authority between parents and children; the concrete difficulties that the family itself experiences in the transmission of values; the growing number of divorces; the scourge of abortion; the ever more frequent recourse to sterilization; the appearance of a truly contraceptive mentality (The Christian Family in the Modern World, no. 6).

FAMILY LIFE

What does the phrase "domestic Church" really mean? In what way is the family the Church?

The phrase "domestic Church" was used by Vatican II only once, in the Dogmatic Constitution on the Church, no. 11. But the expression has been repeated frequently since then. John Paul II summed up its meaning:

> Among the fundamental tasks of the Christian family is its ecclesial task: the family is placed at the service of the building up of the Kingdom of God in history by participating in the life and mission of the Church.

> In order to understand better the foundations, the contents and the characteristics of this participation, we must examine the many profound bonds linking the Church and the Christian family and establishing the family as a "Church in miniature" . . . in such a way that in its own way the family is a living image and historical representation of the mystery of the Church (no. 49).

The threefold office of Jesus (priest, prophet, king) was used by Vatican II to describe the life of the whole people of God. Pope John Paul II used it also to describe the role of families as the domestic Church:

> Having laid the *foundation* of the participation of the Christian family in the Church's mission, it is now time to illustrate its *substance in reference to Jesus Christ as Prophet, Priest and King*—three aspects of a single reality—by presenting the Christian family as (1) a believing and evangelizing community, (2) a community in dialogue with God, and (3) a community at the service of man (no. 50).

What else has the Church done for family life?

One of the prime decisions of the 1980 synod was to endorse the rights of the family. Pope John Paul II summarized these rights as

- the right to exist and progress as a family, that is to say, the right of every human being, even if he or she is poor, to found a family and to have adequate means to support it;

- the right to exercise its responsibility regarding the transmission of life and to educate children;

- the right to the intimacy of conjugal and family life;

- the right to the stability of the bond and of the institution of marriage;

- the right to believe in and profess one's faith and to propagate it;

- the right to bring up children in accordance with the family's own traditions and religious and cultural values, with the necessary instruments, means and institutions;

- the right, especially of the poor and the sick, to obtain physical, social, political and economic security;

- the right to housing suitable for living family life in a proper way;

- the right to expression and to representation, either directly or through associations, before the economic, social and cultural public authorities and lower authorities;

- the right to form associations with other families and institutions in order to fulfill the family's role suitably and expeditiously;

- the right to protect minors by adequate institutions and legislation from harmful drugs, pornography, alcoholism, etc.;

- the right to wholesome recreation of a kind that also fosters family values;

- the right of the elderly to a worthy life and a worthy death;

- the right to emigrate as a family in search of a better life (no. 46).

Marriage and the Nuclear Family: The Christian Ideal

Goals

- To share personal views on important aspects of Christian marriage
- To learn what Vatican II reaffirmed about marriage: It is sacred, it is a sacrament, it fosters human love, and it continues the human race
- To learn what Vatican II said that was new: Marriage is a covenant of life and love, the growth of the spouses is of equal value with procreation of children, and parents are responsible for the size of their families
- To put this learning into practice through action

Scripture

The Christian understanding of marriage has been guided by this classic passage from St. Paul, which speaks of the communion of married love and life.

Ephesians 5:31-33
**"For this reason a man shall leave [his] father and [his] mother
and be joined to his wife,
and the two shall become one flesh."**

This is a great mystery, but I speak in reference to Christ and the church. In any case, each one of you should love his wife as himself, and the wife should respect her husband.

Prayer

God of love and respect, you help us enter the mystery of your life by drawing our attention to the union of husband and wife. Inspire all of us, whatever our state in life, to bear witness to your love by our care and acceptance of one another, as shown in the life of Jesus, our Lord. Amen.

—Based on the prayer from the rite of marriage

Our Experience of Christian Marriage

WHAT WOULD YOU TELL ENGAGED COUPLES?

You are asked to speak to engaged couples in your parish. What is the most important point you want to tell these couples about Christian marriage?

In my view the most important point about Christian marriage is

_____

_____

_____

_____

Some important points mentioned by my partner in this discussion are

_____

_____

_____

_____

Some important points made by Vatican II are

_____

_____

_____

_____

Vatican II Speaks

Vatican II selected the most important points about marriage from the whole Christian tradition and related them to our experience of marriage today. The Pastoral Constitution on the Church in the Modern World states: ''The Council intends to present certain key points of the Church's teaching in a clearer light; and it hopes to guide and encourage Christians and all men who are trying to preserve and to foster the dignity and supremely sacred value of the married state (no. 47).

KEY POINTS

The ''key points'' that the council spoke of are (1) sanctity of marriage, (2) sacrament of marriage, (3) married love, and (4) procreation.

SANCTITY OF MARRIAGE

The first point the council stressed was the sanctity of marriage. Put most simply, marriage is holy because God is the author of marriage. What does this mean?

Vatican II did not go into a theoretical answer to this question but looked instead to the tangible benefits and purposes of marriage, which reveal the hand of God. These are "the continuation of the human race, . . . the personal development and eternal destiny of every member of the family, . . . the dignity, stability, peace, and prosperity of the family and of the whole human race" (no. 48).

SACRAMENT OF MARRIAGE

While not all Christians use the term "sacrament," few Christians would disagree with the way Vatican II described sacramental marriage:

> In virtue of the sacrament of Matrimony by which they signify and share (cf. Eph 5:32) the mystery of the unity and faithful love between Christ and the Church, Christian married couples help one another to attain holiness in their married life and in the rearing of their children. Hence by reason of their state in life and of their position they have their own gifts in the People of God (cf. 1 Cor 7:7) (Dogmatic Constitution on the Church, no. 11).

MARRIED LOVE

Vatican II extolled married love by describing its human qualities and spelling out its religious implications:

> Married love is an eminently human love because it is an affection between two persons rooted in the will and it embraces the good of the whole person; it can enrich the sentiments of the spirit and their physical expression with a unique dignity and ennoble them as the special elements and signs of the friendship proper to marriage. . . .

> Consecrated by Christ's sacrament, this love abides faithfully in mind and body in prosperity and adversity and hence excludes both adultery and divorce. The unity of marriage, distinctly recognized by our Lord, is made clear in the equal personal dignity which must be accorded to man and wife in mutual and unreserved affection. Outstanding courage is required for the constant fulfillment of the duties of this Christian calling (Pastoral Constitution on the Church in the Modern World, no. 49).

PROCREATION

When most people think of marriage and married love, they also think of children. So did Vatican II. "Marriage and married love are by nature ordered to the procreation and education of children. Indeed children are the supreme gift of marriage and greatly contribute to the good of the parents themselves" (no. 50).

Concerning the size of their family, married couples should take into account their own welfare; the welfare of their children; their material and spiritual circumstances; their state of life; the interests of their family, society, and Church; God's laws; and the Church's interpretation of God's laws. "It is the married couple themselves who must in the last analysis arrive at these judgments before God" (no. 50).

Summing Up

Vatican II reaffirmed the sacredness of marriage, which for Catholics is expressed as a sacrament. The new emphasis at Vatican II was on the life and love of the spouses, which included responsibility for regulating family size.

Taking all this into account, the most important thing I learned about Christian marriage is

_____

_____

_____

One way I can put this learning into practice is

_____

_____

_____

Action

To find out about recent Church statements on marriage, I can read The Christian Family in the Modern World, available from the United States Catholic Conference.

To support the Church's view that the relationship of spouses is a top priority, I can find out about marriage preparation and marriage enrichment programs in my parish or diocese, and I can support these programs—with arrangements, advertising, child care, and the like—according to my time and particular talents.

To increase awareness of the forces that work against the sacredness of human love, which is at the heart of the meaning of marriage, I can observe how married love is portrayed in the movies and on television, and I can discuss this with my children and my friends.

Before the Next Session

Carry out one of the Action suggestions.

Complete the "Image of Parenting" exercise on page 26.

Read the section Vatican II Speaks on pages 27–28.

Read the Home Study Questions for Session 3, pages 29–33.

Closing Prayer

O God, in married life you give us a sign of your expectations of us: a holy life nurtured by love in our daily circumstances, transforming ourselves and our world into a gift to place on your altar. In union with all married people may we fulfill your expectations through Christ our Lord. Amen.

—Based on The Christian Family in the Modern World, no. 56

Home Study Questions

HOLINESS OF MARRIAGE

What does it mean to say that God is the author of marriage? Doesn't this religious emphasis detract from the natural goodness of marriage?

At Vatican II the holiness of marriage was attributed to the fact that God is the author of marriage:

> God . . . is the author of marriage and has endowed it with various benefits and with various ends in view: all of these have a very important bearing on the continuation of the human race, on the personal development and eternal destiny of every member of the family, on the dignity, stability, peace, and prosperity of the family and of the whole human race. By its very nature the institution of marriage and married love is ordered to the procreation and education of the offspring and it is in them that it finds its crowning glory (Pastoral Constitution on the Church in the Modern World, no. 48).

If these are the signs of God's authorship, if these are the benefits and purposes that reveal marriage as God intends it, this does not detract from the natural goodness of marriage but draws attention to this goodness from a religious perspective.

Pope John Paul II, drawing on Christian belief in the Trinity, described the universal holiness of marriage in relation to God's love.

> God created man in his own image and likeness: calling him to existence *through love*, he called him at the same time *for love*.

God is love and in himself he lives a mystery of personal loving communion. Creating the human race in his own image and continually keeping it in being, God inscribed in the humanity of man and woman the vocation, and thus the capacity and responsibility, of love and communion. Love is therefore the fundamental and innate vocation of every human being.

As an incarnate spirit, that is, a soul which expresses itself in a body and a body informed by an immortal spirit, man is called to love in his unified totality. Love includes the human body, and the body is made a sharer in spiritual love (The Christian Family in the Modern World, no. 11).

John Paul II went on to elaborate the meaning of such love as it is lived in the partnership of marriage:

Consequently, sexuality, by means of which man and woman give themselves to one another through the acts which are proper and exclusive to spouses, is by no means something purely biological, but concerns the innermost being of the human person as such. It is realized in a truly human way only if it is an integral part of the love by which a man and a woman commit themselves totally to one another until death. The total physical self-giving would be a lie if it were not the sign and fruit of a total personal self-giving, in which the whole person, including the temporal dimension, is present: if the person were to withhold something or reserve the possibility of deciding otherwise in the future, by this very fact he or she would not be giving totally (no. 11).

This teaching does not detract from the natural goodness of marriage; rather, it offers a vision that in fact enhances that natural goodness.

MARRIAGE AS A SACRAMENT

What makes a marriage a sacrament, and what difference does that make?

The basis for considering marriage a sacrament is the baptism of the spouses. The difference it makes is understood in terms of the relationship of Jesus and the Church, which is uniquely experienced in marriage.

Receiving and meditating faithfully on the word of God, the Church has solemnly taught and continues to teach that the marriage of the baptized is one of the seven sacraments of the New Covenant.

Indeed, by means of baptism, man and woman are definitively placed within the new and eternal covenant, in the spousal covenant of Christ with the Church. And it is because of this indestructible insertion that the intimate community of conjugal life and love, founded by the Creator, is elevated and assumed into the spousal charity of Christ, sustained and enriched by his redeeming power (no. 13).

The revised Code of Canon Law makes the same point:

The matrimonial covenant, by which a man and a woman establish between themselves a partnership of the whole of life, is by its nature ordered toward the good of the spouses and the procreation and education of the offspring; this covenant between baptized persons has been raised by Christ the Lord to the dignity of a sacrament (can. 1055).

For this reason a matrimonial contract cannot validly exist between baptized persons unless it is also a sacrament by that fact (can. 1055).

MARRIED LOVE

What's so special about **Christian** *married love? When you get right down to it, sex is sex.*

Vatican II stressed two points about Christian married love: It is fully human and it simultaneously participates in God's love. For this reason married love is to be exalted, not reduced to a matter of mere physical attraction.

A love like that, bringing together the human and divine, leads the partners to a free and mutual giving of self, experienced in tenderness and action, and permeates their whole lives; besides, this love is actually developed and increased by the exercise of it. This is a far cry from mere erotic attraction, which is pursued in selfishness and soon fades away in wretchedness (Pastoral Constitution on the Church in the Modern World, no. 49).

Pope Paul VI restated this view in his Encyclical Letter on the Regulation of Births:

The characteristic features and exigencies of married love are clearly indicated, and it is of the highest importance to evaluate them exactly.

This love is above all fully *human*, a compound of sense and spirit. It is not, then, merely a question of natural instinct or emotional drive. It is also, and above all, an act of the free will, whose dynamism ensures that not only does it endure through the joys and sorrows of daily life, but also that it grows, so that the husband and wife become in a way one heart and one soul, and together attain their human fulfillment (no. 9).

Parenting: Creating the Domestic Church

Goals

- To share personal views about the roles of parents
- To recall what Vatican II said about Christian parents: They are responsible for the size of their family, for the education of their children, and for creating an environment in which the family develops
- To learn what Vatican II said that was new: The family is "the Church in miniature," "the domestic Church," and parents' responsibilities have social implications
- To put this learning into practice through action

Scripture

This Scripture passage expresses God's desire that parents hand on their experience and faith to their children.

Deuteronomy 4:9-10 "Take care and be earnestly on your guard not to forget the things which your own eyes have seen, nor let them slip from your memory as long as you live, but teach them to your children and to your children's children: There was the day on which you stood before the LORD, your God, at Horeb, and he said to me, 'Assemble the people for me; I will have them hear my words, that they may learn to fear me as long as they live in the land and may so teach their children.'"

Prayer

Loving God, Creator of the universe, maker of man and woman in your likeness, source of blessing for married life, we humbly pray to you for all spouses and parents.

May your fullest blessing come upon them so that they may together rejoice in your gift of married love.

Lord, may they praise you when they are happy and turn to you in their sorrows. May they be glad that you help them in their work and know that you are with them in their need.

May they pray to you in the community of the Church and be your witnesses in the world. May they reach old age in the company of their friends and come at last to the kingdom of heaven.

We ask this through Christ our Lord. Amen.

—Based on the nuptial blessing

Our Experience of Parenting

IMAGES OF PARENTING

Sometimes it's difficult to really express the full meaning of our most important experiences. Using images from the everyday world or the world of nature, try to capture the deep meaning of parenting.

You can write a short paragraph, list words or phrases, draw a picture, or create a symbolic drawing (food, water, an ear, a cradle, a handshake, a guide—whatever expresses the depth of parenting for you). Remember, there are no ''correct'' meanings of parenting. Each person's experience is valid.

Vatican II
Speaks

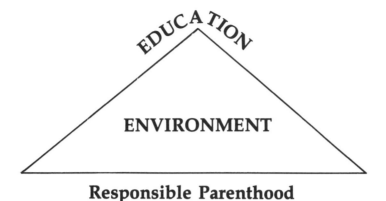

Responsible Parenthood

RESPONSIBLE PARENTHOOD

The basic right and responsibility of married people is to establish a family. This is not done arbitrarily. Married people are expected to take into account all those items we talked about last time—their own welfare; the welfare of their children; their material and spiritual circumstances; their state of life; the interests of their family, society, and Church; God's laws; and the Church's interpretation of God's laws.

Pope Paul VI said in his Encyclical Letter on the Regulation of Births that "the commitment to responsible parenthood requires that husband and wife, keeping a right order of priorities, recognize their own duties toward God, themselves, their families and human society" (no. 10).

EDUCATION

Having children is not the end of parental responsibility. "As it is the parents who have given life to their children, on them lies the gravest obligation of educating their family. They must therefore be recognized as being primarily and principally responsible for their education" (Declaration on Christian Education, no. 3).

To carry out the responsibility of educating their children, parents must be free to choose schools. Governments must support parents and protect children's right to education, and parents and educational authorities must strive for the development of the whole child even as adults continue their own lifelong learning.

ENVIRONMENT

In addition to formal education through schooling, parents also develop their children by providing a family environment that can be described as "the Church in miniature" or "the domestic Church."

"It is . . . the duty of parents to create a family atmosphere inspired by love and devotion to God and their fellow-men which will provide an integrated, personal and social education of their children" (no. 3).

The council picked up on this theme in its Decree on the Apostolate of Lay People:

> The mission of being the primary vital cell of society has been given to the family by God himself. This mission will be accomplished if the family, by the mutual affection of its members and by family prayer, presents itself as a domestic sanctuary of the Church; if the whole family takes its part in the Church's liturgical worship; if, finally, it offers active hospitality, and practices justice and other good works for the benefit of all its brothers suffering from want" (no. 11).

Summing Up

Vatican II reaffirmed parents' responsibility for the size, education, and environment of the family. The new emphasis at Vatican II was on the family as a domestic Church and on creating an environment that goes with it.

In order to bring this discussion into our daily life, finish this statement:

To me, being a Christian parent means

_____

_____

_____

Action

To learn more about the Church's view of Christian parenthood, I can read Pope Paul VI's Encyclical Letter on the Regulation of Births or Pope John Paul II's apostolic exhortation The Christian Family in the Modern World, both available from the United States Catholic Conference.

To help provide the support that parents need in carrying out their responsibilities, I can see what the parish or diocese offers in this area; I can volunteer to help, according to my time or particular talents; if there is a need, I can start a parents' support group.

To help parents in their primary responsibility—that of educating their children—I can volunteer to help in the school or religious education program as a teacher, aide, or the like, according to my own gifts.

Before the
Next Session

Complete the "Interview" exercise on pages 34–35.

Closing Prayer

O Loving God, when you created human beings, you willed that husbands and wives should be one. Bless all married people and make their love fruitful so they may be living witnesses to your divine love in our world. Amen.

—Based on the opening prayer of the Wedding Mass

Home Study
Questions

PROCREATION

Are Catholics supposed to have as many children as possible?

For a long time the official teaching of the Catholic Church gave the impression that this was the sole purpose of marriage or certainly the primary aim to which all other aims were subordinate.

Vatican II did not want to perpetuate this view; neither did it want to lessen the value of having children. It formulated its position this way:

> Without intending to underestimate the other ends of marriage, it must be said that true married love and the whole structure of family life which results from it is directed to disposing the spouses to cooperate valiantly with the love of the Creator and Savior, who through them will increase and enrich his family from day to day (Pastoral Constitution on the Church in the Modern World, no. 50).

The Council recognized that the responsibility for making decisions about having children rests with married couples. Far from advocating parents having as many children as physically possible, Vatican II set forth the role married couples must play in regulating the size of their families.

> Married couples should regard it as their proper mission to transmit human life and to educate their children; they should realize that they are thereby cooperating with the love of God the Creator and are, in a certain sense, its interpreters. This involves the fulfillment of their role with a sense of human and Christian responsibility and the formation of correct judgments through docile respect for God and common reflection and effort (no. 50).

But doesn't the Church make regulation of family size impossible for married couples by not allowing birth control?

The Church's official position on birth control was summed up by Pope Paul VI.

Responsible parenthood . . . refers to the objective moral order instituted by God—the order of which a right conscience is the true interpreter. As a consequence the commitment to responsible parenthood requires that husband and wife, keeping a right order of priorities, recognize their own duties toward God, themselves, their families, and human society (Encyclical Letter on the Regulation of Births, no. 10).

Regarding the means of limiting family size,

the sexual activity, in which husband and wife are intimately and chastely united with one another, through which human life is transmitted, is . . . "honorable and good." It does not . . . cease to be legitimate even when, for reasons independent of their will, it is foreseen to be infertile. For its natural adaptation to the expression and strengthening of the union of husband and wife is not thereby suppressed. The facts are, as experience shows, that new life is not the result of each and every act of sexual intercourse. God has wisely ordered the laws of nature and the incidence of fertility in such a way that successive births are already naturally spaced. . . . The Church, nevertheless, in urging men to the observance of the precepts of the natural law, . . . teaches as absolutely required that *in any use whatever of marriage* there must be no impairment of its natural capacity to procreate human life (no. 11).

Specifically,

if therefore there are reasonable grounds for spacing births, arising from the physical or psychological condition of husband or wife, or from external circumstances, the Church teaches that then married people may take advantage of the natural cycles . . . and use their marriage at precisely those times that are infertile, and in this way control birth, a way that does not in the least offend the moral principles (no. 16).

EDUCATION

When the Church stresses education so much, is it because the Church really wants to control people and education is one of the best ways to do that?

In Church documents education refers to the whole development of a person, with freedom and dignity at the core. If anything, the education the Church endorses helps people recognize and overcome forms of control that would unfairly limit their freedom and violate their dignity.

All men of whatever race, condition or age, in virtue of their dignity as human persons, have an inalienable right to education. This education should be suitable to the particular destiny of individuals, adapted to their ability, sex and national cultural traditions, and should be conducive to fraternal relations with other nations in order to promote true unity and peace in the world. True education is directed towards the formation of the human person in view of his final end and the good of that society to which he belongs and in the duties of which he will, as an adult, have a share (Delcaration on Christian Education, no. 1).

Of all the resources available to parents, the school is the most valuable. The Declaration on Christian Education discusses the role of the school, both public and parochial.

In nurturing the intellectual faculties which is its special mission, [the school] develops a capacity for sound judgment and introduces the pupils to the cultural heritage bequeathed to them by former generations. It fosters a sense of values and prepares them for professional life. By providing for friendly contacts between pupils of different characters and backgrounds it encourages mutual understanding. Furthermore it constitutes a center in whose activity and growth not only the families and teachers but also the various associations for the promotion of cultural, civil and religious life, civic society, and the entire community should take part (no. 5).

John Paul II expanded on this notion:

Even amid the difficulties of the work of education, difficulties which are often greater today, parents must trustingly and courageously train their children in the essential values of human life. Children must grow up with a correct attitude of freedom with regard to material goods, by adopting a simple and austere life style and being fully convinced that "man is more precious for what he is than for what he has."

In a society shaken and split by tensions and conflicts caused by the violent clash of various kinds of individualism and selfishness, children must be enriched not only with a sense of true justice, which alone leads to respect for the personal dignity of each individual, but also and more powerfully by a sense of true love, understood as sincere solicitude and disinterested service with regard to others, especially the poorest and those in most need (The Christian Family in the Modern World, no. 37).

The dignity of children is clearly set forth:

In the family, which is a community of persons, special attention must be devoted to the children, by developing a profound esteem for their personal dignity, and a great respect and generous concern for their rights. This is true for every child, but it becomes all the more urgent the smaller the child is and the more it is in need of everything, when it is sick, suffering or handicapped (no. 26).

Traditionally, the mother has had the primary responsibility for raising the children. Does the Church still think it is this way?

Vatican II saw the role of raising the children to be equally and fully shared by both parents and consistently spoke in the plural when discussing parental responsibility.

John Paul II made this point in his discussion of fatherhood:

> Love for his wife as mother of their children and love for the children themselves are for the man the natural way of understanding and fulfilling his own fatherhood. Above all where social and cultural conditions so easily encourage a father to be less concerned with his family or at any rate less involved in the work of education, efforts must be made to restore socially the conviction that the place and task of the father in and for the family is of unique and irreplaceable importance. As experience teaches, the absence of a father causes psychological and moral imbalance and notable difficulties in family relationships, as does, in contrary circumstances, the oppressive presence of a father, especially where there still prevails the phenomenon of "machismo," or a wrong superiority of male prerogatives which humiliates women and inhibits the development of healthy family relationships (no. 25).

Are Catholics still expected to send their children to parochial schools?

Vatican II affirmed the value of Catholic schools, but at the same time recognized the limitations parents face in taking advantage of them. "Catholic parents are reminded of their duty to send their children to Catholic schools whenever this is possible, to give Catholic schools all the support in their power, and to cooperate with them in their work for the good of their children" (Declaration on Christian Education, no. 8).

Canon Law makes the same statement: "Parents are to entrust their children to those schools in which Catholic education is provided; but if they are unable to do this, they are bound to provide for their suitable Catholic education outside the schools" (can. 798).

How can the Church help married people fulfill these responsibilities?

John Paul II summarized the view of the 1980 synod by speaking of pastoral care of families. In general, the Church sees itself as a companion, assisting families as they need help.

> Like every other living reality, the family too is called upon to develop and grow. After the preparation of engagement and the sacramental celebration of marriage, the couple begin their daily journey towards the progressive actuation of the values and duties of marriage itself.

In the light of faith and by virtue of hope, the Christian family too shares, in communion with the Church, in the experience of the earthly pilgrimage towards the full revelation and manifestation of the Kingdom of God.

Therefore, it must be emphasized once more that the pastoral intervention of the Church in support of the family is a matter of urgency. Every effort should be made to strengthen and develop pastoral care for the family, which should be treated as a real matter of priority, in the certainty that future evangelization depends largely on the domestic Church (The Christian Family in the Modern World, no. 65).

Youth: Recipients or Contributors?

Goals

- To share the feelings of the group about youth today, based on interviews with young people
- To recall what Vatican II said about youth in terms of their contributions and their formation for political, cultural, and married life
- To learn what was new in Vatican II's approach: that youth have a contribution to make and that they also have a special peer ministry
- To put this learning into practice through action

Scripture

Like Timothy, young people today have a contribution to make. And like St. Paul, parents must hand on the ways of God to their children.

1 Timothy 4:12-15 Let no one have contempt for your youth, but set an example for those who believe, in speech, conduct, love, faith, and purity. . . . Do not neglect the gift you have, which was conferred on you through the prophetic word with the imposition of hands of the presbyterate. Be diligent in these matters, be absorbed in them, so that your progress may be evident to everyone.

Prayer

O God, ever new and creative, bless young people everywhere. They are the hope of the Church and the world on the verge of the year 2000. Through them fill us with youthful energy to prepare our world for the coming of your kingdom, through Christ our Lord. Amen.

—Based on The Christian Family in the Modern World, no. 86

Our Experience of Youth

INTERVIEW

Adults are often inclined to simply stand back, observe, and judge young people. How often do we take the time to really know them— who they are, what they think, how they feel?

To prepare for this discussion, interview a young person between the ages of fifteen and twenty.

34

Do not interview a member of your own family.

The key questions to ask are

What is your biggest concern?

_____

_____

_____

_____

What is your greatest hope?

_____

_____

_____

_____

What does the Church mean to you?

_____

_____

_____

_____

Notes/comments from this interview

_____

_____

_____

_____

Notes/comments from the others' interviews

_____

_____

_____

_____

Concern	Hope	Church
_____	_____	_____
_____	_____	_____
_____	_____	_____
_____	_____	_____

_____

_____

_____

Vatican II Speaks

Vatican II didn't really say much about young people, probably because many of the urgent problems today's youth face weren't foreseen, for example, drugs, AIDS, and suicide.

But one problem Vatican II did acknowledge was the so-called generation gap.

> A change in attitudes and structures frequently calls accepted values into question. This is true above all of young people who have grown impatient at times and, indeed, rebellious in their distress. Conscious of their own importance in the life of society, they aspire to play their part in it all the sooner. Consequently, it frequently happens that parents and teachers face increasing difficulties in the performance of their tasks (Pastoral Constitution on the Church in the Modern World, no. 7).

CONTRIBUTIONS OF YOUTH

Young people are much more than rebels causing grief to their elders. The council acknowledged their special gifts as it pointed out two areas in which young people have an important role to play: that of the lay apostolate and that of peer ministry:

> The growth of their social importance demands from them a corresponding apostolic activity; and indeed their natural character inclines them in this direction. Carried along by their natural ardor and exuberant energy, when awareness of their own personality ripens in them they shoulder responsibilities that are theirs and are eager to take their place in social and cultural life. . . . The young should become the first apostles of the young, in direct contact with them, exercising the apostolate by themselves among themselves, taking account of their social environment (Decree on the Apostolate of Lay People, no. 12).

FORMATION OF YOUTH

Every person, youth or adult, has to be prepared in order to contribute.

In the area of cultural life,

> education . . . has its source and its cradle, as it were, in the family: there, children in an atmosphere of love learn more quickly the true scale of values, and approved forms of culture are almost naturally assimilated by the developing minds of adolescents (Pastoral Constitution on the Church in the Modern World, no. 61).

In the area of political life,

> so that all citizens will be able to play their part in political affairs, civil and political education is vitally necessary for the population as a whole and for young people in particular, and must be diligently attended to (no. 75).

In the area of married life,

> it is imperative to give suitable and timely instruction to young people, above all in the heart of their own families, about the dignity of married love, its role and its exercise; in this way they will be able to engage in honorable courtship and enter upon marriage of their own (no. 49).

Summing Up

Vatican II recognized the eagerness of young people to play a part in society, which sometimes causes tension with elders.

The new emphasis at Vatican II was to urge the active role of youth in the life of the Church, as well as to underscore the importance of their formation for life in society.

In light of this discussion,

Do I see youth primarily as older children (recipients) or as young adults (contributors)?

_____

_____

One way I can put this learning into practice is

_____

_____

Action

With heightened sensitivity to the dignity of all people, I can spend more time with my own teenagers. I can also spend time talking with other teenagers—treating them as persons of worth, respecting their ideas and opinions.

To stimulate participation of youth in the Church, I can find out how well young people are represented in parish organizations, including the parish council, and I can encourage such representation.

To support programs in which youth help one another, I can volunteer to help with peer ministry programs, youth programs, and retreats.

Before the Next Session

Carry out one of the Action suggestions.

Read the Case Study in Session 5, pages 40–41. Then write your answer to the question about divorce.

Read your section of Vatican II Speaks.

Read the Home Study Questions for Session 5, pages 44–47.

Closing Prayer

O abiding Spirit of God, keep our generations united. Help the elders among us to pass on faithfully the light of wisdom and the sureness of experience. Move young people to respond energetically to the world they inherit and the future they shape. And show us the ways we can work together for your glory, through Christ our Lord. Amen.

—Based on the closing message of Vatican II to youth

Special Marriage Situations: Annulment, Divorce, Remarriage

Goals

- To examine the description of the ideal family in Church documents
- To learn how the Church views families who don't meet the ideal, for example, through divorce, interfaith marriage, and remarriage after divorce
- To clarify what these families may and may not do in the Church
- To put this learning into practice through action

Scripture

Jesus was once confronted by a single parent who was not of his people. His response to her guides our response to families in special situations.

Matthew 15:21-28 **Then Jesus went from that place and withdrew to the region of Tyre and Sidon. And behold, a Canaanite woman of that district came and called out, ''Have pity on me, Lord, Son of David! My daughter is tormented by a demon.'' But he did not say a word in answer to her. His disciples came and asked him, ''Send her away, for she keeps calling out after us.'' He said in reply, ''I was sent only to the lost sheep of the house of Israel.'' But the woman came and did him homage, saying, ''Lord, help me.'' He said in reply, ''It is not right to take the food of the children and throw it to the dogs.'' She said, ''Please, Lord, for even the dogs eat the scraps that fall from the table of their masters.'' Then Jesus said to her in reply, ''O woman, great is your faith! Let it be done for you as you wish.'' And her daughter was healed from that hour.**

Prayer

O God, you invite all people to eat at the one table of your love. With you we long for the day when this will come about. Until then, help us to unite ourselves with others in every way possible as a preparation for the full union of all members in the one body of Christ, our Lord. Amen.

—Based on *Admitting Other Christians to Eucharistic Communion in the Catholic Church*

*Our View
of Special
Marriage
Situations*

FACTS ABOUT DIVORCE, ANNULMENT, AND REMARRIAGE

Because some of the questions on page 41 have factual answers, the following information will be helpful when the discussion begins:

1. A divorced person can receive Communion. The fact of a civil divorce does not exclude a Catholic from Communion. This is because the Catholic Church does not acknowledge a civil divorce as ending the marriage bond.

2. If a divorced Catholic remarries and has not received an annulment of the first marriage, that person may not receive Communion. An annulment is a Church declaration that the necessary conditions for marriage were not present at the time of the marriage; therefore, no marriage took place.

3. A couple whose marriage is not approved by the Church may attend Mass but not receive Communion. Such couples are actually encouraged to attend Mass for the spiritual benefit it offers. Whether these couples should take an active, public role in other activities of the parish is a question which calls for a prudent pastoral response. Ordinarily, it is desirable to involve people as much as possible.

4. Catholics and Protestants may be married in a Catholic church according to the Catholic rite of marriage. Such marriages do not ordinarily take place within the celebration of Mass. This is to avoid any awkwardness about who may receive Communion.

   With permission, Catholics may be married in a Protestant church. Ordinarily the Protestant minister presides, and a Catholic priest or deacon may offer some prayers or blessings.

   When a Catholic and a Protestant marry, the Catholic is instructed to do everything possible to have the children baptized and raised as Catholics. The Protestant is informed of the Catholic's responsibilities but is not obliged to make any promises or commitments. In practice, the couple must make the decision about the religious upbringing of their children.

CASE STUDY

After Mass one Sunday during coffee and donut time you overhear this conversation:

Parishioner A: I couldn't believe it! Mary Ann Smith going to Communion just as proud as you please! Everyone knows she just got her divorce last week.

Parishioner B: Being divorced doesn't mean you can't go to Communion. If she remarries, then she can't go to Communion.

Parishioner A: Well, that's just a matter of time, I can tell you! And when she does remarry, I bet she still goes to Communion!

Parishioner B: I'll tell you who I feel sorry for. Sue and Bob Franklin. They are the nicest young couple, but he was married once before and their request for an annulment was turned down, so they can't go to Communion.

Parishioner A: If you want my opinion, this annulment business is just a sham anyway. There shouldn't be annulments and there shouldn't be divorce. People should stick by their commitments.

Parishioner B: But sometimes there are circumstances that call for an annulment. Why penalize someone unnecessarily?

Parishioner A: Who's being penalized? The Franklins come to Mass and they're accepted by everyone. I'll tell you who was penalized—I was. When I married a Protestant thirty years ago, we couldn't have a Church wedding. We never did feel welcome in the parish.

Parishioner B: You certainly don't want to return to that, do you?

Parishioner A: No, but we need some standards. We need to know what it means to be a Catholic today.

If you were to join this conversation, how would you answer these questions:

Is parishioner B correct that a divorced person can receive Communion?

If Mary Ann does remarry, can she still receive Communion?

Are Sue and Bob Franklin allowed to attend Mass? Can they do anything else in church?

Can a Catholic and a Protestant be married in the Catholic Church today? What obligations do they have to each other and to their children?

Is parishioner A's attitude in line with Vatican II? Why do you think parishioner A has the views that were expressed?

How do you think Catholics should respond to people who are divorced, separated, remarried after divorce, in a mixed marriage?

Our group consensus is

_____

_____

_____

Vatican II
Speaks

NUCLEAR FAMILIES

Vatican II used the word "family" in different ways. John Paul II did the same: "In matrimony and in the family a complex of interpersonal relationships is set up—married life, fatherhood and motherhood, filiation and fraternity—through which each human person is introduced into the 'human family' and into the 'family of God,' which is the Church" (The Christian Family in the Modern World, no. 15).

Both the council and the Pope almost always had the nuclear family in mind when they referred to the family: two parents in a lifelong marriage, children at home, the father working to support the family, and the mother caring for the children and the household.

But perhaps half the Catholics in the United States do not live in such a family. This poses a challenge for the whole Church.

DIVORCE AND SEPARATION

The biggest challenge to the ideal family is divorce. Vatican II said little except that divorce shouldn't happen between Christian spouses. John Paul II said more.

Regarding separated spouses:

Loneliness and other difficulties are often the lot of separated spouses, especially when they are the innocent parties. The ecclesial community must support such people more than ever. It must give them much respect, solidarity, understanding and practical help, so that they can preserve their fidelity even in their difficult situation; and it must help them to cultivate the need to forgive which is inherent in Christian love, and to be ready perhaps to return to their former married life (no. 83d).

Regarding divorced spouses:

The situation is similar for people who have undergone divorce, but, being well aware that the valid marriage bond is indissoluble, refrain from becoming involved in a new union and devote themselves solely to carrying out their family duties and the responsibilities of Christian life. In such cases their example of fidelity and Christian consistency takes on particular value as a witness before the world and the Church. Here it is even more necessary for the Church to offer continual love and assistance, without there being any obstacle to admission to the sacraments (no. 83d).

Regarding divorced persons who have remarried:

Pastors and the whole community of the faithful [should] help the divorced, and with solicitous care . . . make sure that they do not consider themselves as separated from the Church, for as baptized persons they can, and indeed must, share in her life. They should be encouraged to listen to the word of God, to attend the Sacrifice of the Mass, to persevere in prayer, to contribute to works of charity and to community efforts in favor of justice, to bring up their children in the Christian faith, to cultivate the spirit and practice of penance and thus implore, day by day, God's grace. Let the Church pray for them, encourage them and show herself a merciful mother, and thus sustain them in faith and hope (no. 84).

It is clear that John Paul II wanted to do everything possible to affirm divorced people and their families.

However, neither the sacrament of reconciliation nor Eucharist can be extended so long as the remarried persons stay together as husband and wife.

Summing Up   Vatican II reaffirmed the permanence of sacramental marriage. John Paul II and the 1980 synod on the family addressed the special needs of separated, divorced, and remarried Catholics, urging their support and participation in the Church to the extent possible.

For me, the most important learning of the last five sessions is

_____

_____

_____

Action   To put this learning into practice for myself and for the group, I will spend 15 minutes in the coming week thinking about and completing this statement:

One activity the group could perform to put this into practice is

_____

_____

_____

Before the Next Session   Complete the above Action.

Closing Prayer O God, share with us your compassion for families in special situations. Make us sensitive to the needs of single parents, migrants, those forced apart by war and imprisonment, or damaged by drug and alcohol abuse. Keep us mindful that the future of humanity passes the way of the family, and help us do everything we can to prepare that way according to your desires, through Christ our Lord. Amen.

—Based on The Christian Family in the Modern World, nos. 77, 86

Home Study Questions ## MIXED MARRIAGES

Protestants don't recognize marriage as a sacrament, and yet their marriages are considered sacramental by the Catholic Church. Why is that? Doesn't that impose a Catholic view on other Christians?

Baptism is the basis for the sacrament of marriage. In the current ecumenical age the Catholic Church presumes the baptism of other Christian Churches is valid. Therefore, the marriage of validly baptized Christians, whether they are Catholic or not, is sacramental.

Vatican II stated the official view of the Church on this matter in its Decree on Ecumenism: ''By the sacrament of Baptism, whenever it is properly conferred in the way the Lord determined and received with the proper dispositions of soul, man becomes truly incorporated into the crucified and glorified Christ and is reborn to a sharing of the divine life'' (no. 22).

In one sense this position may seem to impose a Catholic view on other Christians. But it should be remembered that other Christians are not expected to carry out all the duties of Catholics, even if they marry Catholics.

The Catholic Church respects the integrity and differences of other Churches, but at the same time it must respect the integrity of baptism. And since baptism is the basis for the sacrament of marriage, the marriage of baptized Christians is a sacrament.

What are the obligations if a Catholic marries a Protestant? Have these changed since Vatican II?

Today, especially in light of the ecumenical development, the expectations of Catholics who marry Christians of another tradition are quite different from the expectations before Vatican II.

In general, these marriages are still referred to as ''mixed marriages,'' implying a mixture of Christian traditions. They are also called ''ecumenical'' or ''interfaith'' marriages.

The focus of responsibility is on the Catholic rather than the non-Catholic. The other Christian spouse is to be informed of the Catholic's responsibilities.

Mixed marriages are viewed as special situations and still require the permission of the local bishop. The wedding ceremony is expected to take place in a Catholic church, although the bishop may give permission for the wedding to take place in the church of the other Christian spouse.

Pope John Paul II summarized these points in his exhortation The Christian Family in the Modern World:

> Couples living in a mixed marriage have special needs, which can be put under three main headings.
>
> In the first place, attention must be paid to the obligations that faith imposes on the Catholic party with regard to the free exercise of the faith and the consequent obligation to ensure, as far as is possible, the Baptism and upbringing of the children in the Catholic faith.
>
> There must be borne in mind the particular difficulties inherent in the relationships between husband and wife with regard to respect for religious freedom: this freedom could be violated either by undue pressure to make the partner change his or her beliefs, or by placing obstacles in the way of the free manifestation of these beliefs by religious practice.
>
> With regard to the liturgical and canonical form of marriage, Ordinaries can make wide use of their faculties to meet various necessities.
>
> In dealing with these special needs, the following points should be kept in mind:
>
> - In the appropriate preparation for this type of marriage, every reasonable effort must be made to ensure a proper understanding of Catholic teaching on the qualities and obligations of marriage, and also to ensure that the pressures and obstacles mentioned above will not occur.
>
> - It is of the greatest importance that, through the support of the community, the Catholic party should be strengthened in faith and positively helped to mature in understanding and practicing that faith, so as to become a credible witness within the family through his or her own life and through the quality of love shown to the other spouse and the children.
>
> Marriages between Catholics and other baptized persons have their own particular nature, but they contain numerous elements that could well be made good use of and developed, both for their intrinsic value and for the contribution that they can make to the ecumenical movement. This is particularly true when both parties are faithful to their religious duties. Their common Baptism and the

dynamism of grace provide the spouses in these marriages with the basis and motivation for expressing their unity in the sphere of moral and spiritual values (no. 78).

The Code of Canon Law pinpoints the obligations of the Catholic:

> The Catholic party declares that he or she is prepared to remove dangers of falling away from the faith and makes a sincere promise to do all in his or her power to have all the children baptized and brought up in the Catholic Church.

> The other party is to be informed at an appropriate time of these promises which the Catholic party has to make, so that it is clear that the other party is truly aware of the promise and obligation of the Catholic party.

> Both parties are to be instructed on the essential ends and properties of marriage which are not to be excluded by either party (can. 1125).

Fulfilling Christian married love is not easy and certainly not automatic. But each Christian couple contributes to the achievement of other couples by fulfilling as much as possible the ideal of married love.

> Authentic married love will be held in high esteem, and healthy public opinion will be quick to recognize it, if Christian spouses give outstanding witness to faithfulness and harmony in their love, if they are conspicuous in their concern for the education of their children, and if they play their part in a much needed cultural, psychological, and social renewal in matters of marriage and the family (Pastoral Constitution on the Church in the Modern World, no. 49).

ANNULMENT AND DIVORCE

What about annulments? Aren't they really divorces? It is a well-known fact that Catholic marriages end in divorce as often as other marriages. So isn't all this talk about Christian married love just meaningless idealism?

Annulments are not the same as divorce. An annulment declares that a valid marriage never actually existed. It is a judgment in hindsight, while divorce is a declaration that a valid marriage existed but was terminated by the will of the spouses.

It is true that Catholics do obtain civil divorces, but these are not recognized by the Catholic Church. They do not dissolve the marriage. Consequently, a divorced Catholic is not free to marry another person.

Because the Catholic Church does not recognize divorce, a Catholic who is divorced civilly is not prevented by that fact from participating in the life of the Church, including the sacraments.

However, just because it does not recognize civil divorce, the Church, especially the local parish, should not disregard the pain and disruption and needs of divorced persons. Too often there is a stigma attached to divorce and a lack of support for those who experience it.

The positions spelled out by John Paul II in The Christian Family in the Modern World, nos. 83d and 84, are in tension with prevailing attitudes and practices in the United States as well as with the views of other Christian Churches. They are consistent, however, with the understanding of married love as set forth in official Church teaching.

The Family of God: Now What?

Goals

- To formulate the consensus of the group about what they have learned in the previous sessions
- To determine whether the group wants to carry out an action that will put their learning into practice
- To celebrate in prayer the sharing of the last five sessions

Scripture

Everyone who hears the word of God is expected to put it into practice.

James 1:22-25 **Be doers of the word and not hearers only, deluding yourselves. For if anyone is a hearer of the word and not a doer, he is like a man who looks at his own face in a mirror. He sees himself, then goes off and promptly forgets what he looked like. But the one who peers into the perfect law of freedom and perseveres, and is not a hearer who forgets but a doer who acts, such a one shall be blessed in what he does.**

Prayer

O God, who spoke and the world was created, who promised and the covenant was fashioned, who came and people were saved, do not let us become forgetful listeners, but help us to put your word into practice, now and all the days of our life. Amen.

Learning into Action

1. Go back to page 43 and read your statements about your own learning and a possible group action.

2. Write those statements with any changes you now wish to make on the following lines:

Statement of Learning	*Proposed Action*
_____	_____
_____	_____

_____   _____

_____   _____

3. Designate one person to write each person's responses (from the lines above) on a sheet of tablet paper.

4. When everyone's responses have been recorded, study them for a few moments.

5. Has more than one person mentioned the same learning or the same action? If so, the designated person puts one check beside this response for each person who mentioned it.

6. If the response with the most checks is agreeable to everyone, allowing for minor additions or changes, this is the consensus of the group.

7. If there is no common response or if none is agreeable to the group, is there a way to combine some of the responses? Take your time in doing this.

8. If a combined statement is suggested, the designated person writes it on the tablet. Is it agreeable to everyone, allowing for minor changes or additions? If so, this is the consensus of the group.

9. If no consensus on anything is possible, then this is the result of the group's deliberation.

10. Designate one person from each subgroup to report the consensus to the large group.

SUBGROUP DISCUSSIONS

Notes/comments from this discussion, including the subgroup's consensus Statement of Learning and Proposed Action.

_____

_____

_____

_____

_____

_____

LARGE GROUP DISCUSSION

Statement of Learning   *Proposed Action*

(Group 1 Consensus)

_____   _____

_____   _____

_____   _____

(Group 2 Consensus)

_____   _____

_____   _____

_____   _____

Notes/comments

_____

_____

_____

FINAL CONCENSUS

Statement of Learning   *Proposed Action*

_____   _____

_____   _____

_____   _____

LOOKING AHEAD

A group action is highly recommended as a conclusion to this program, *Families;* however, the decision for or against a group action is entirely up to the group.

To help the group or part of the group develop the action proposal into a working plan and carry it out, the optional session, "Learning into Action," follows.

The optional session goes beyond the convener's commitment to *Vatican II: Act II.* The convener may agree to continue, or a new convener must be chosen.

If a group action is to be carried out, three subgroups should be formed to decide on (1) the basis in Vatican II for the intended action, (2) what must be done to accomplish the action, and (3) what the intended outcome is to be.

Each person should read the section Preparing for Action, stay in touch with their subgroup to exchange ideas and information, and bring their written ideas to the session.

Write the final consensus Statement of Learning and Proposed Action on page 54 in your booklet.

Scripture and Closing Prayer

Tobit 13:13-16

Go, then, rejoice over the children of the righteous,
  who shall all be gathered together
  and shall bless the Lord of the ages.
Happy are those who love you,
  and happy those who rejoice in your prosperity.

Happy are all the men who shall grieve over you,
  over all your chastisements,
For they shall rejoice in you
  as they behold all your joy forever.

My spirit blesses the Lord, the great King;
  Jerusalem shall be rebuilt as his home forever.
Happy for me if a remnant of my offspring survive
  to see your glory and to praise the King of heaven!

What have the last six sessions meant to me?

_____

_____

_____

How am I different because of these sessions?

_____

_____

_____

Mark 3:31-35 **His mother and his brothers arrived. Standing outside they sent word to him and called him. A crowd seated around him told him, ''Your mother and your brothers [and your sisters] are outside asking for you.'' But he said to them in reply, ''Who are my** mother and [my] brothers?'' And looking around at those seated in the circle he said, ''Here are my mother and my brothers. [For] whoever does the will of God is my brother and sister and mother.''

Exchange a greeting of peace.

Learning into Action: An Optional Exercise

Preparing for Action

Read this Preparing for Action section, talk to other members of your subgroup, and bring your written ideas to the session.

A meaningful and satisfying group action should be well planned. In the *Vatican II: Act II* program the essential ingredients for a well-planned action are the following:

Statement of learning: This is the final consensus Statement of Learning from page 50.

For example, the group's consensus statement might be that "Young people should be treated like contributors rather than recipients."

Proposed action. This is the final consensus Proposed Action statement from page 50.

For example, "A young adult between the ages of fifteen and twenty should be elected to serve on every parish committee."

Basis in Vatican II. This includes the chapters in specific documents where the basis for the Statement of Learning and Proposed Action can be found.

Plan of action. This is a list of steps needed to accomplish the action.

For example, in the case of involving young people in the parish government, the group could decide to

1. meet with the youth group and its leaders to get their reactions and suggestions,
2. meet with the parish council to propose a concrete plan for proceeding,
3. meet with the pastor and parish council to discuss changes in bylaws, if that is necessary,
4. recruit young people for the next parish election,
5. run a series of articles in the parish newsletter on the importance of young people's contributions,
6. publicize testimony of adults about the value of young people's participation and contributions.

For each item, the group decides what resources are needed, who is responsible, and when each step will be completed.

Intended outcome. This identifies the specific outcome the group plans to accomplish. The group should make sure that the goal is realistic.

For example, what organizations *must* have a youth representative, in the group's opinion? Are there organizations that would be inappropriate?

What percentage of parish organizations with a youth representative would constitute success for this action?

Prayer

Begin the session with this Prayer.

O God of patience and hope, you urge us to think creatively, to act courageously, and to trust confidently. When we make the smallest effort, you bless it generously; and when we are unable to act together, you give us more time. Stay with us as we spread the benefits of what we have learned to others. We ask this through Christ our Lord. Amen.

Developing the Action

(20 minutes) Write in the final consensus Statement of Learning and Proposed Action from Session 6, page 50.

Statement of Learning	*Proposed Action*
_____	_____
_____	_____
_____	_____
_____	_____

The subgroups should meet for a few minutes to finalize their statements.

Basis in Vatican II

Ask subgroup 1 to describe the Basis in Vatican II which they developed. All should record their findings on the lines below.

_____

_____

_____

Plan of Action

Ask subgroup 2 to describe their Plan of Action. All should record the subgroup's plan.

Specific steps:_____

_____

_____

_____

Resources needed:_____

_____

_____

_____

People responsible:_____

_____

_____

_____

Time frame:_____

_____

_____

_____

Intended Outcome

Ask subgroup 3 to report their Intended Outcome. Record the Intended Outcome below.

_____

_____

_____

_____

SUBGROUP DISCUSSIONS

(20 minutes) The subgroups should now separate. Each subgroup will discuss among themselves the findings or proposals of another subgroup.

The convener will spend time with each subgroup, answer questions, and keep the subgroups aware of the time.

Basis in Vatican II

Do the passages selected establish the basis for the action agreed to?

_____

_____

Are there other passages you would recommend?_____

_____

_____

Plan of Action

Can the specific actions be carried out?_____

_____

_____

Will they achieve the goal?_____

_____

_____

Would you suggest others?_____

_____

_____

Are the necessary resources available?_____

_____

_____

Are other resources needed?_____

_____

_____

Is it clear who is responsible for each step?_____

_____

_____

Is the time frame realistic?_____

_____

_____

Intended Outcome

Is the intended outcome clear?_____

_____

_____

Are the standards for judging success easily recognizable?_____

_____

_____

Is the time for completing the project realistic?_____

_____

_____

(10 minutes) Break

When the large group has reconvened, ask each subgroup to add their insights to the original findings and proposals. Members of the large group may want to comment, either on the original findings and proposals or on the new insights gained from the subgroup discussions.

REFINING THE PLAN

(20 minutes) Each subgroup should now meet to discuss the new ideas gained and to refine their part of the proposed action. This will be the Final Plan.

At the end of this time, the subgroups should present the Final Plan to the entire group, and everyone should record it on the lines below.

Final Plan

Basis in Vatican II

_____

_____

_____

_____

Plan of Action

_____

_____

_____

_____

Intended Outcome

_____

_____

_____

_____

If any member, following his or her own best judgment in the light of Vatican II, has reservations about any part of the plan, these should be discussed now. The particular member may choose to work with the group despite the reservations or may choose to do something else.

Likewise, if the group has been unable to agree about the plan as a whole, this should not be judged a failure. It is simply a fact. The learning and the sharing of different viewpoints and values should be affirmed and celebrated.

Closing Prayer

After a moment of silence to feel God's presence, recite this Closing Prayer together.

O gracious God, we give you thanks that we have spent this time together. May we use every opportunity you give us to spread your word and nourish your life in others as we work for the coming of your kingdom, through Christ our Lord. Amen.

Reviewing the Action

If the action is to be carried out, group members will be in close contact with one another during that period of time. When the action has been completed, it is recommended that the group come together one last time to learn from each other about the experience and to celebrate this action carried out in the spirit of Vatican II.

The following questions may help guide your reflection.

Overall, how do I feel about our group's action?

_____

_____

_____

_____

_____

How do I feel about my part in it?

_____

_____

_____

_____

_____

What could we have done differently that would have made it more successful?

_____

_____

_____

_____

_____

What was the best thing that happened as a result of the project?

_____

_____

_____

_____

_____

What did I learn from this project about myself?

_____

_____

_____

_____

_____

about Vatican II?

_____

_____

_____

_____

_____

about the topic **Families?**

_____

_____

_____

_____

_____

Summary

Marriage is a communion of life and love that shares in the life and love of God.

Christians, blessed through their baptism in their life in Jesus, share in that life in a special way in marriage, which is expressed as a sacrament.

Married couples are responsible for deciding about the size of their families and the spacing of their children, in harmony with God's intentions and the belief of the Church as formulated by the Pope and the bishops.

The family is a domestic Church, sharing in its own special way in the priestly, prophetic, and pastoral roles of Jesus.

Married people and families are the primary ministers to one another. They should be free to form associations to advocate for their rights and for the satisfaction of their needs.

The Church, as the family of God, is understood best in relation to the domestic family, the prime model for all other uses of the term ''family.''

The Vatican II Documents

The Constitution on the Sacred Liturgy (Sacrosanctum Concilium)

Two guiding principles govern the restoration of rites for sacraments and Liturgy of the Hours: revisions should lead to the full, conscious, and active participation of the faithful and rites should be simple and intelligible.

Dogmatic Constitution on the Church (Lumen Gentium)

The Church is a sign of the mystery of God's life in the world; the Church consists of all the baptized; all are called to holiness and have a role to play in the mission of the Church, although in different ways; Mary is the model and mother of the Church.

Dogmatic Constitution on Divine Revelation (Dei Verbum)

There is one revelation of God which comes through the twin sources of Scripture and Tradition; Scripture should be central in the daily life of the faithful, venerated equally with the Eucharist.

Pastoral Constitution on the Church in the Modern World (Gaudium et Spes)

The Church has a distinctive contribution to make to human dignity, human community, and human activity by interpreting the signs of the times in light of the gospel; the Church gives to and receives from society in seeking solutions to urgent problems.

Decree on the Means of Social Communication (Inter Mirifica)

Modern communications media are valuable aids in linking people together and spreading the gospel.

Decree on the Catholic Eastern Churches (Orientalium Ecclesiarum)

The Churches of the East are respected for their distinctive rites, theological emphases, and spiritual contributions; Catholics of the West may share their sacraments.

Decree on Ecumenism *(Unitatis Redintegratio)*

Catholic participation in ecumenism is guided by the belief that the fullness of Christ's Church subsists in the Roman Catholic Church; Protestant Churches and communities are a means of grace and salvation; Catholics are partly responsible for divisions with Protestants; every effort at every level should be made to achieve unity, although sharing the Eucharist is not yet possible; Catholics should develop an ecumenical spirit without compromising or misrepresenting the truth.

Decree on the Pastoral Office of Bishops in the Church *(Christus Dominus)*

Bishops have collegial bonds with one another and the Pope; the bishop's primary duty is to proclaim God's word; bishops have responsibility to the universal Church, the national Church, and their own diocese.

Decree on the Training of Priests *(Optatam Totius)*

Priestly training should be pastoral; the whole Church is involved in vocation recruitment and support.

Decree on the Up-to-Date Renewal of Religious Life *(Perfectae Caritatis)*

Religious orders should revise their constitutions by returning to the charism of their founder, taking account of modern conditions, and involving all their members.

Decree on the Apostolate of Lay People *(Apostolicam Actuositatem)*

The laity's distinct role is in society although they have the right and duty to use their gifts in the Church also; there are many forms and areas of the lay apostolate; spiritual formation and preparation for lay activity are essential.

Decree on the Church's Missionary Activity *(Ad Gentes Divinitus)*

The Church is missionary by nature; the primary forms of its mission activity are witness, preaching and worship, community; the whole Church should cooperate in carrying out missionary activity.

Decree on the Ministry and Life of Priests *(Presbyterorum Ordinis)*

The priest is a representative of the bishop and shares collegial bonds with other priests; the priest's primary role is to preach the word and celebrate the sacraments; the ministry is the main source of a priest's spirituality.

Declaration on Christian Education *(Gravissimum Educationis)*

Every person has a right to education; parents have a right to determine the education of their children; governments and Churches should help parents exercise their rights.

Declaration on the Relation of the Church to Non-Christian Religions *(Nostra Aetate)*

God's truth and grace are found in other religions; this is the basis for cooperation and dialogue; Jews have a special relationship with Christians and should not be held responsible for the death of Jesus.

Declaration on Religious Liberty *(Dignitatis Humanae)*

Modern awareness of human dignity and freedom of conscience coincide with God's revelation; no one should be prevented from worshiping according to conscience or be forced to worship against conscience.

The complete documents of Vatican II are available in *Vatican Council II: The Conciliar and Post Conciliar Documents,* Austin Flannery, ed. (Collegeville: The Liturgical Press, 1987).

Other documents referred to in this book and written after the council are available in *Vatican Council II: More Post Conciliar Documents,* Austin Flannery, ed. (Collegeville: The Liturgical Press, 1982).

Individual documents may be purchased from the United States Catholic Conference, 3211 Fourth St. N.E., Washington, DC 20017-1194.